Here Comes Charlie Brown!

Selected Cartoons from
GOOD 'OL CHARLIE BROWN Vol. II

Charles M. Schulz

CORONET BOOKS
Hodder Fawcett Ltd., London

Coronet edition 1970
Second Impression 1971
Third Impression 1972
Fourth Impression 1973

Printed and bound in Great Britain for
Coronet Books,
Hodder Fawcett Ltd,
St. Paul's House, Warwick Lane,
London, EC4P 4AH
by Hazell Watson & Viney Ltd,
Aylesbury, Bucks

ISBN 0 340 12618 3

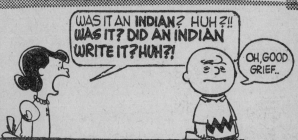

LUCY, HOW DID YOU EVER GET TO BE SUCH A FUSS-BUDGET?

I'LL HAVE YOU KNOW I STUDIED HARD! LOOK AT ALL THOSE BOOKS.. EACH ONE A COURSE IN ITSELF...

"FROM RAGS TO FUSS-BUDGET".. "THE POWER OF POSITIVE FUSSING".. "GREAT FUSS-BUDGETS OF OUR TIME"..

AND HERE'S ONE OF MY REAL FAVORITES..." I WAS A 'FUSS-BUDGET FOR THE F.B.I.'"!

ZOOM!

NOW, YOU CUT THAT OUT!

SCHULZ

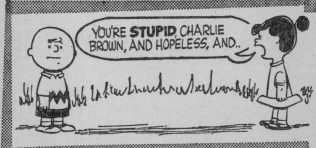

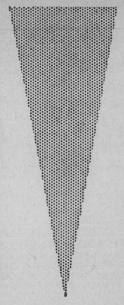

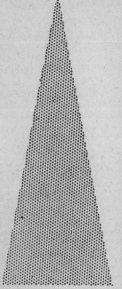

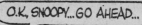

THAT'S BEAUTIFUL SCHROEDER.. WHAT IS IT?

THE FIRST PRELUDE AND FUGUE FROM 'THE WELL-TEMPERED CLAVICHORD' BY BACH..

IT'S BEAUTIFUL ANYWAY..

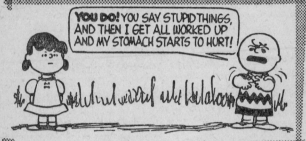

THOSE DUMB KIDS! I'LL BET IF I WERE A POLAR BEAR, THEY'D NEVER THROW SNOWBALLS AT ME!

IF I WERE A POLAR BEAR, I'D WALK RIGHT OVER TO THEM, AND I'D..

SCHULZ

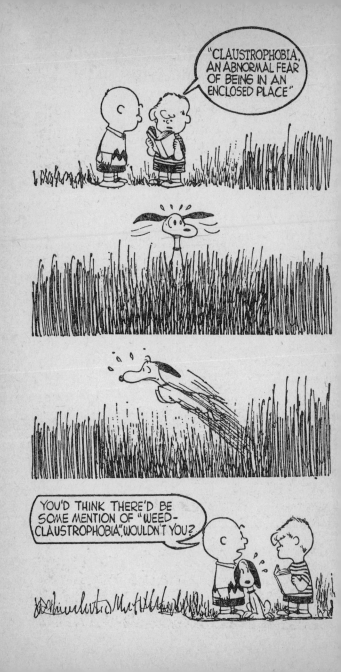

KLUNK!
BUMP!
BUMP!
bumpety-bump
CRASH!!

WHAT IN THE WORLD WAS **THAT**?!

I GUESS IT WAS SNOOPY..IF HE DOESN'T LIKE HIS SUPPER, HE JUST PUSHES IT DOWNSTAIRS!

YOU SURE SEE A LOT OF AIR CONDITIONERS AROUND THESE DAYS..

ALMOST ALL THE STORES AND OFFICES HAVE THEM..

AND EVEN QUITE A FEW HOMES, TOO..

UH HUH..

SNOOPY

SCHULZ

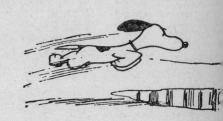

© 1970 United Feature Syndicate, Inc.

Wherever Paperbacks Are Sold

OTHER 'PEANUTS' TITLES IN CORONET BOOKS

*All these books are available at your bookshop or newsagent, or can b
ordered direct from the publisher. Just tick the titles you want and fill
the form below.*

CORONET BOOKS, Cash Sales Department, P.O. Box 11, Penry
Cornwall.

Please send cheque or postal order. No currency, and allow 7p per boo
(6p per book on orders of five copies and over) to cover the cost o
postage and packing in U.K., 7p per copy overseas.

Name..

Address..

....